21st Century
Junior Library

INFOGRAPHICS:
BUDGETING

Econo-Graphics Jr.

Christina Hill

Published in the United States of America by:

CHERRY LAKE PUBLISHING GROUP
Ann Arbor, Michigan
www.cherrylakepublishing.com

Reading Adviser: Beth Walker Gambro, MS, Ed., Reading Consultant, Yorkville, IL
Photo Credits: Cover: Marta Shershen/Getty Images; Page 1: ©Marta Shershen/Getty Images; Page 7: ©Visual Generation Inc./Getty Images; Page 13: ©Valeriia Soloveva/Getty Images; Page 14: ©franckreporter/Getty Images; Page 15: ©Jaen Zevallos/Pixabay, ©REDQUASAR/Pixabay, ©Clker-Free-Vector-Images/Pixabay, ©Clker-Free-Vector-Images/Pixabay, ©Harisankar Sahoo/Pixabay, ©sumit kumar/Pixabay, ©Mohamed Hassan/Pixabay; Page 17: ©nadia_bormotova/Getty Images

Cherry Lake Press is an imprint of Cherry Lake Publishing Group.

Library of Congress Cataloging-in-Publication Data
Names: Hill, Christina, author.
Title: Infographics. Budgeting / Christina Hill.
Other titles: Budgeting
Description: Ann Arbor, Michigan : Cherry Lake Publishing, [2023] | Series: Econo-graphics Jr. | Includes bibliographical references and index. | Audience: Grades 2-3 | Summary: "Why is it important to understand budgeting? In the Econo-Graphics Jr. series, young readers will examine economy-related issues from many angles, all portrayed through visual elements. Income, budgeting, investing, supply and demand, global markets, inflation, and more are covered. Each book highlights pandemic-era impacts as well. Created with developing readers in mind, charts, graphs, maps, and infographics provide key content in an engaging and accessible way. Books include an activity, glossary, index, suggested reading and websites, and a bibliography"— Provided by publisher.
Identifiers: LCCN 2022037940 | ISBN 9781668919262 (hardcover) | ISBN 9781668920282 (paperback) | ISBN 9781668919262 (pdf) | ISBN 9781668921616 (ebook)
Subjects: LCSH: Finance, Personal—Juvenile literature. Classification: LCC HG179 .H4697 2023 | DDC 332.024—dc23/eng/20220912
LC record available at https://lccn.loc.gov/2022037940
Cherry Lake Publishing Group would like to acknowledge the work of the Partnership for 21st Century Learning, a network of Battelle for Kids. Please visit http://www.battelleforkids.org/networks/p21 for more information.

Printed in the United States of America
Corporate Graphics

Before embracing a career as an author, **Christina Hill** received a bachelor's degree in English from the University of California, Irvine, and a graduate degree in literature from California State University, Long Beach. When she is not writing about various subjects from sports to economics, Christina can be found hiking, mastering yoga handstands, or curled up with a classic novel. Christina lives in sunny Southern California with her husband, two sons, and beloved dog, Pepper Riley.

CONTENTS

WHAT IS A BUDGET?

A **budget** is a plan for money.

The goal is to balance **income** and **expenses**. Income is money that is earned. Expenses are things that money is spent on.

A Balanced Budget

Expenses

$5 discount movie ticket

$2 sports drink at the Snack Shack

$5 baseball

Income

$23 savings

$10 weekly allowance

$10 birthday money

$10 for walking the neighbor's dog

$5 for washing Grandpa's car

Budget

INCOME AND EXPENSES

It starts with income. Children can get allowances or gifts. Employees get **wages.**

Businesses also need money. Many get **loans** from banks.

The government gets money from **taxes**.

Fast Facts

Most Americans spend their money on housing, transportation, and food.

According to the U.S. Bureau of Labor Statistics (as of 2020), each month the average American spends:

- $1,784 on housing
- $819 on transportation
- $610 on food

How Americans Spend Their Money

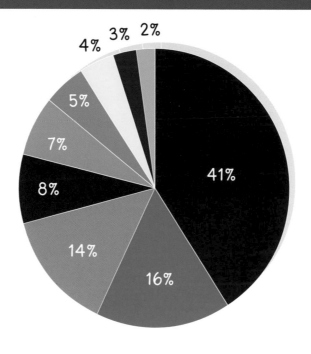

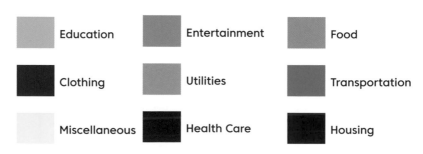

2017. U.S. Bureau of Labor Statistics

FEDERAL AND STATE BUDGETS

In the United States, the president creates a budget.

The government gets most of its income from taxes. Taxes are collected on what people earn, buy, and own.

Where the U.S. Federal Government Gets Money

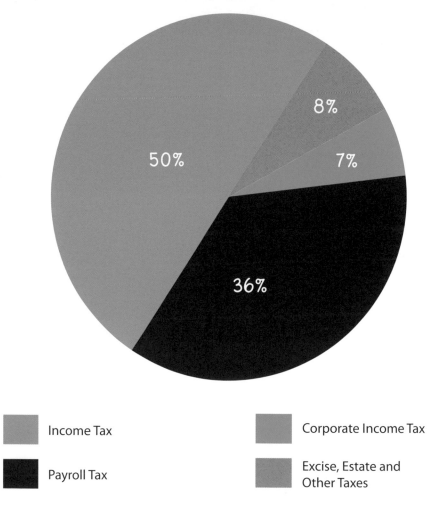

50%

8%

7%

36%

Income Tax

Corporate Income Tax

Payroll Tax

Excise, Estate and Other Taxes

2019, Center on Budget and Policy Priorities

What the U.S. Federal Government Spends Money On

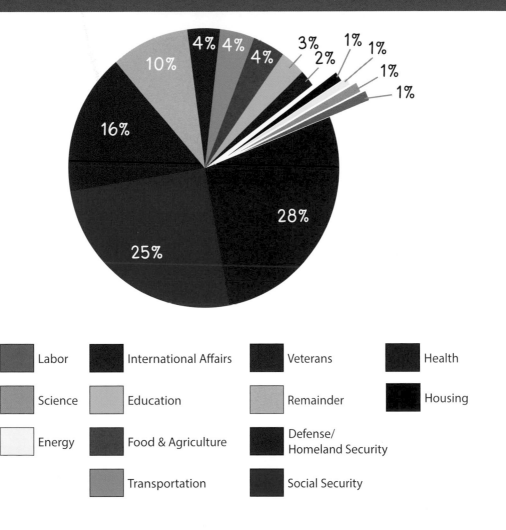

■ Labor	■ International Affairs	■ Veterans	■ Health
■ Science	■ Education	■ Remainder	■ Housing
■ Energy	■ Food & Agriculture	■ Defense/ Homeland Security	
	■ Transportation	■ Social Security	

2015, Poynter Institute

WANTS VS. NEEDS

A budget needs balance. Think about wants and needs. Needs come first. Wants come second.

Food and housing are needs. Everyone also has things they want.

Wants vs. Needs

Things that are wanted but not needed to survive	VS.	Things needed to survive
Changes over time	VS.	Does not change
Different for all people	VS.	Same for all people

In a budget, half of your income should be for needs.

Dividing the Budget Pie

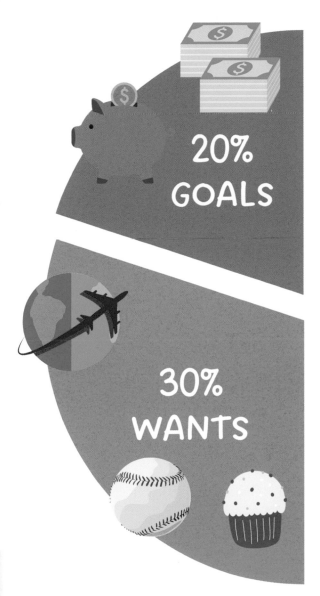

20% GOALS

30% WANTS

50% NEEDS

BUILDING A BUDGET

The goal is to have a *balanced* budget. It should have room for needs, wants, and savings. **Debt** happens when someone spends more than they earn and save.

Budgets are different for everyone. Not everyone has the same wants. Income can change.

The number one rule:

SPEND LESS THAN YOU EARN!

Calculating Debt-to-Income Ratio

Monthly debt divided by monthly income equals
a debt-to-income (DTI) ratio.

Debt-to-Income Ratio Ranges

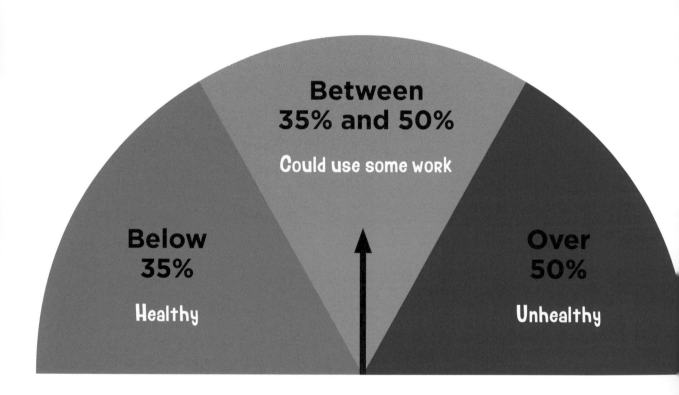

Between
35% and 50%

Could use some work

Below
35%

Healthy

Over
50%

Unhealthy

How Much Have You Saved?

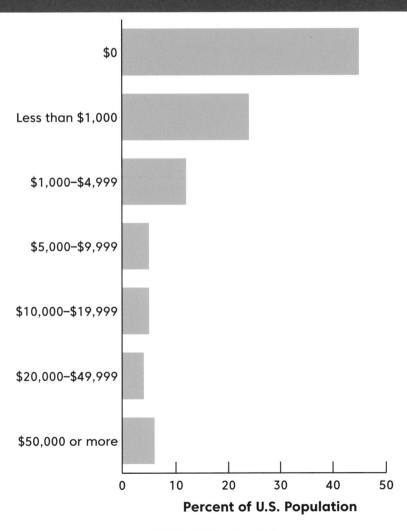

	Percent of U.S. Population
$0	
Less than $1,000	
$1,000–$4,999	
$5,000–$9,999	
$10,000–$19,999	
$20,000–$49,999	
$50,000 or more	

Percent of U.S. Population

2019, GO BankingRates

How to Build a Budget

Set a Budget Goal

How much money are you trying
to save each month?

List Your Income

How much money do you
gain each month?

List Your Expenses

Note that this amount may
change each month.

Set Aside Savings

Remember your budget goal when saving.

Track Everything

A dollar here or there will add up quickly! Subtract everything you spend from your earnings.

Adjust

Continue to adjust the budget as needed to meet goals.

ACTIVITY
Create a Balanced Budget

Your big sister just got her first job. She wants your help to make a budget. Her goal is to save $300 each month for 6 months. Her monthly income is $1,200. Her monthly expenses include her car payment of $200. She spends $100 on gas. She spends $300 on food and clothing.

Here are a few things to keep in mind:

In August, your family is going on vacation. Your sister wants to budget $50 for T-shirts and $300 for a surfboard.

In September, she wants to go to a concert. The ticket costs $50.

Your sister's birthday is in November. Your grandma always sends her $100.

Create a chart to help your sister track her money. How much will she have left over? How much money should she start saving each month?

Month	Description	Income	Expenses	Balance
July				
August				
September				
October				
November				
December				

LEARN MORE

Books

...akers, Diane. *The Bottom Line: Money Basics*. New York: Crabtree Publishing, 2017.

...nden, Cecilia. *Living on a Budget*. New York: Smartbook Media Inc., 2017.

Websites

...ritannica Kids: Budget
...tps://kids.britannica.com/students/article/budget/273391

...e Mint: Fun for Kids
...ww.themint.org/kids

...ibliography

...hatzky, Jean. "*Five Things You Need to Know About Money*." April 29, 2021. https://...ww.timeforkids.com/partner/pwc/g4/five-things-you-need-to-know-about-money

...ockert, Melanie. "*What Is Economic Surplus and How Does It Work?*" July 21, 2022. ...tps://www.businessinsider.com/personal-finance/surplus-definition

... Shea, Bev, and Lauren Schwahn. "*Budgeting 101: How to Budget Money*." May 18, ...022. https://www.nerdwallet.com/article/finance/how-to-budget

...ohwinkle, Jeremy. "*How to Make a Personal Budget in 6 Easy Steps*." Last modified ...nuary 24, 2022. https://www.thebalance.com/how-to-make-a-budget-1289587

GLOSSARY

budget (BUH-juht) amount of money available for spending based on a plan for how it will be spent

debt (DET) amount of money that you owe a person, bank, or company

expenses (ik-SPEN-sehz) amounts of money needed to pay for and buy things

income (IN-kuhm) money received for work or through investments on a regular basis

loans (LOHNZ) amounts of money that are given to someone with a promise that they will be paid back

taxes (TAKS-ehz) amount of money that a government requires citizens to pay that is used to fund the things the government provides for them

wages (WAYJ-ehz) amount of money that a worker is paid based on the time worked

INDEX